W9-ANN-575

THE GIFT OF LOVE

Text written and compiled by Marion Stroud
Produced in conjunction with Tony Stone Photolibrary

HARPER & ROW, PUBLISHERS, SAN FRANCISCO
Cambridge, Hagerstown, New York, Philadelphia
London, Mexico City, São Paulo, Sydney

The Gift of Love.
Copyright © 1981 by Lion Publishing.
All rights reserved. No part of this book may be used or reproduced in any manner
whatsoever without written permission except in the case of brief quotations embodied
in critical articles and reviews. For information address Harper & Row, Publishers, Inc.,
10 East 53rd Street, New York, NY 10022. Published simultaneously in Canada by
Fitzhenry & Whiteside, Limited, Toronto.

FIRST U.S. EDITION

Acknowledgments
All pictures supplied by Tony Stone Photolibrary,
28 Finchley Road, St John's Wood, London NW8 6ES.

Bible quotations as follows: Song of Songs 8:6-7, Matthew 18:21-22, 1 Corinthians
13:4-8a, 1 John 4:18 from *Good News Bible*, copyright 1966, 1971 and 1976 American
Bible Society; published by Bible Societies/Collins; Luke 6:36-38, 1 Corinthians 13:7,
14:1, Galatians 5:13-14, 22-23a from *The Living Bible*, copyright 1971 Tyndale House
Publishers.

Copyright material as follows: 'Journey of discovery' and 'To walk in beauty' by
Marjorie Holmes from *A time to love*, published by The C. R. Gibson Company, 1976;
'The three words' and 'I believe in you' by Fred Bauer from *For rainy Mondays and other
dry spells*, published by Prometheus Press, 1973; 'The six most important words' from
For women only, published by Tyndale House Publishers, 1974; 'You are the trip I did
not take' from *The sun is high* by Rita Snowden, published by Hodder and Stoughton,
1974; 'A gift from God' and 'Believing in love' by Ulrich Schaffer from *Love reaches out*,
published by Harper & Row, 1976; 'For love, brave love that ventureth' by
Amy Carmichael from *Edges of his ways*, published by Christian Literature
Crusade, 1955.

Every effort has been made to trace and contact copyright owners. If there are any
inadvertent omissions in the acknowledgments, we apologize to those concerned.

Printed in Italy by New Interlitho S.P.A., Milan

LC: 81-47903

ISBN: 0-06-067752-X

82 83 84 85 86 10 9 8 7 6 5 4 3 2 1

Love is a feeling to be learned.

It is tension and fulfillment.

It is deep longing and hostility.

It is gladness and it is pain.

There is not one without the other.

Happiness is only a part of love—this is what
has to be learned. Suffering belongs to love
also. This is the mystery of love, its beauty and
its burden.

Love is a feeling to be learned.

Walter Trobisch

LOVE IS...

Love is longing for you to telephone and then feeling scared when you do in case I say the wrong thing.

Love is feeling sad when you have gone away and yet glad because you will enjoy the trip.

Love is misery when we quarrel, happiness when we understand each other, loneliness when you're away.
Love is knowing all about you and loving you just the same.

We need no teacher to help us fall in love or out of love, but the art of loving must be learned.

Falling in love is largely a matter of expecting your partner to fulfill your own expectations.

Falling out of love comes about when he or she fails to fulfill them.

The art of loving involves acknowledging reality and adjusting to it.

BETTER THAN DREAMS

With my dream lover, I ran barefoot on the beach.
I sat and listened while he played his guitar
and murmured love songs in the moonlight.

My dream world was full of laughter and freedom,
Sunny days and starlit nights,
Suppers in style and surprise presents.

Reality is looking out for you at the bus-stop;
Holding the tools when you work on the car;
Cold winter winds, shopping on Saturdays,
Lunch with Auntie Grace,
And going out to dinner on payday.

TELL ME

Something is bothering you. Please share it with me. Please tell me how you feel. Your face has its 'closed-in' look, like a window with the curtains drawn. I watch you, but I can see nothing of what is going on inside.

Is there trouble with your boss? Is your Dad getting at you again? Has your Mom said something about us? Perhaps you wish that you were watching football on television instead of being here with me. Maybe you wish that I would vanish and that another girl would take my place!

Something is wrong, and I want to help you. To be with you in it. To share the bad times as well as the good. But how can I know unless you tell me? Please tell me how you feel.

'There is no fear in love; perfect love drives out all fear.'

1 John 4:18

THE REAL ME

If I should tell you what I really feel, would you still love me? If I should open the door to my secret self and let you look inside, would you be shocked? Or worse still, would you laugh?

If you knew that I am scared of your Mom, believe in God and want six children, would it make any difference to you?

There are dreams that I dream that I have never wanted to share with anyone—until now. There are fears that crawl round and round in my mind when it is dark that seem silly in the morning. Perhaps you could banish them for ever—if you knew what they were.

Should I tell you what I really feel? If I share my feelings with you like this I take a risk. A risk that you could use this knowledge to hurt me, to humiliate me, and so to destroy our love. But with the risk there comes a possibility. The possibility that such knowledge could bind us together, because our love is built on trust and understanding and reality.

JOURNEY
OF DISCOVERY.

*Every experience in love is a journey
of self discovery. The more we
learn about the one we love, the more we
learn about ourselves. And even though
the love may cool and we may go our
separate ways, we have gained in
knowledge. We understand at least one
other person better. And we cannot help
but better understand that intriguing,
groping, puzzling companion we are
destined to live with for ever: the secret
inner self.*

Marjorie Holmes

SPACE TO GROW

Where the Spirit of the Lord is,
there is freedom.

2 Corinthians 3:17

'Don't try to own him!' That is what Dad said
last night, when I had stopped crying for long
enough to tell him. I thought that he would see
it my way. Agree that you should want to be
with me all the time, just as I want to be with
you.

Instead he took your side. Oh! he lent me
his hanky, like he used to do when I was a kid,
and he patted me on the shoulder. But he took
your side when he said 'Let him have his own
life sometimes. A man needs space to be
himself.'

'Space to be yourself.' Do you really need
that? Do I? Space to grow; space to develop;
space for others?

Is my love strong enough to allow for that
space? For real love must always walk hand in
hand with freedom.

JUST THE WAY YOU ARE

It is half past seven and you're late again. This is the fourth time this month that you've been late. The fourth time that I have stood on this corner, watching, waiting, listening to the church clock ticking away the minutes— every minute seeming like an hour.

You promised it wouldn't happen again. You said you would leave early; shut your eyes and ears to other people's problems. So what is keeping you tonight? What is making you late again?

The film will be starting now. The others have gone inside. 'Come in with us!' they said. 'Be gone when he gets here. That'll bring him to his senses!'

But I'll wait on the corner a little bit longer. I'll wait while you give some of 'our' time to others, because that's the way you are. 'Three weeks late at birth,' your Mom says, 'and late ever since. Too kind-hearted for his own good.'

But I love your kindness, so I'll try to greet you with a smile whether you are late or early. Perhaps next time you will be on time. And today I'll wait a little longer.

I AM SORRY

'Peter came to Jesus and asked, "Lord, if my brother keeps on sinning against me, how many times do I have to forgive him? Seven times?" "No, not seven times," answered Jesus, "but seventy times seven." '

Matthew 18:21-22

*The three words
which keep Romeos and Juliets in glory
are not 'I love you'
but 'I am sorry'*

Fred Bauer

Tickets for a concert. Such a silly thing to have a fight about. But we did agree that every little bit helps if we are ever going to get a place of our own. We said that we would save; cut out the luxuries. And then you bought tickets for a concert.

I wish that I could call them back. Those awful things that I shouted at you. Flinging words like knives; wanting to hurt you like you had hurt me. I wish that I had not brought your mother into it, or the girl you used to know. I wish that you had not slammed out of the house without saying goodnight.

Last night I was hot with anger and hurt. This morning I am cold. Cold and frightened. It is not the first time that we have quarrelled. Will you ever come back? How can I bridge the gap between us? Will 'sorry' be enough?

'IT IS IN GIVING THAT WE RECEIVE'

I snapped at you when you phoned this
morning and I'm sorry. I was tired of not
being able to afford new clothes; seeing you
once during the week because you're working
overtime or going to college; sympathizing
when you feel low. I wanted someone to fuss
over *me* for a change!

I had to be by myself for a while. To get
away from people and noise and love songs
on the radio. So I slipped into the church I
pass on the way to work. And that was where
I saw it. A golden scroll that glowed against
those gray stone walls, just like sunshine. And
on it were words from the Bible:

'Try to show as much compassion as your Father does,' it said. 'Never criticize or condemn—or it will all come back on you. Go easy on others; then they will do the same for you. For if you give you will get! Your gift will return to you in full and overflowing measure, pressed down, shaken together to make room for more, and running over. Whatever measure you use to give—large or small—will be used to measure what is given back to you.'

'If you give you will get!' You wouldn't have thought that there were down-to-earth things like that in the Bible, would you? It is hard to accept and harder still to do all those things. I'd like to have a copy of that scroll for us. Then one day we can put it up in our own home. But tonight I want to say that I'm sorry and I love you.

Love ever gives, forgives, outlives,
Love ever stands with open hands,
And while it lives, it gives.
For this is Love's prerogative
To give and give and give and give.

The six most important words—
I am sorry, I was wrong
The five most important words—
You did it very well
The four most important words—
What do you think?
The three most important words—
I love you
The two most important words—
Thank you
The one most important word—
We

The least important word—
I

I
APPRECIATE
<u>YOU</u>

'There is always one who kisses, and one who holds the cheek.'

Oh God, why is it that I find it so hard to tell him how I feel? When I am alone, I think of all the things I love about him: his crooked smile, the look in his eyes, and his hands, so gentle and yet so strong. I love his sense of humor too, and the way that he really listens to what I have to say.

I can talk to the girls at work about him by the hour. And yet when I am in his arms and he whispers compliments into my ear, all that I can say is 'I love you too!'

'I love you.' It says it all, and yet it says so little. Please help me to show my admiration. To tell him how attractive I find him. To give him the appreciation and the encouragement that we all want. After all, I love it when he praises me! Set me free from my shyness, embarrassment and fear of saying the wrong thing. Let me take my turn at being the one who kisses; giving without wanting to get — like you do.

How do I love thee? Let me count the ways.
  I love thee to the depth and breadth and height
  My soul can reach, when feeling out of sight
For the end of Being and ideal Grace.
I love thee to the level of everyday's
  Most quiet need, by sun and candlelight.
  I love thee freely, as men strive for Right;
I love thee purely, as they turn from Praise.
I love thee with the passion put to use
  In my old griefs, and with my childhood's faith.
I love thee with a love I seemed to lose
  With my lost saints, —I love thee with the breath,
Smiles, tears, of all my life!—and, if God choose,
  I shall but love thee better after death.

Elizabeth Barrett Browning

LOVING
AND GIVING

'Love is not just an emotion to be felt, but an attitude to be acted upon.'

'How can you be sure that this is the real thing?' she asked me. 'Remember the other times? What makes you think that this love will last?'

Trust my sister to bring up awkward questions like that! But she *has* made me wonder. How *do* you know when you have found the right person to spend the rest of your life with? How can you be sure that love

will last? My grandmother had some advice to offer when I asked her. She is a very wise old lady, my grandmother.

'Love thinks of the other person first,' she said. 'Wants the very best for them and acts lovingly even when it does not feel like it. If you love someone you see them with their bad points as well as their good ones, and love them just the same. You share the fun and you share the dull days. You feel the same whether he is with you or away; up to his eyes in mud or all dressed up for a party. And it's not so much what you *say* as what you *do*.

'Loving is sometimes moonlight and roses. But mostly it means giving. It's being willing to put his interests first; not in one great self-sacrificial flourish, but in the little things, day after day after day. To love in that way, you need help from God, the Source of Love. But if you can face the thought of that kind of loving and giving, then you have found the real thing.'

WHEN LOVE GROWS UP

Love and sacrifice are woven together—
inseparable strands in the fabric of our lives.

Sacrifice makes love grow up. Children
love, but their love is impatient, possessive,
demanding immediate fulfillment. Grown-up
love is able to wait, to share, to understand.

To sacrifice means to put aside one's
own needs and pleasures for the good of
another. It is learning to say 'ours' and 'we'
instead of 'yours' and 'mine'.

Giving up rights, possessions and time
is not always joyful. It is an art to be learned,
and there is a price to be paid. But the art of
giving up and letting go is the most important
art to be learned. The cost is high but the
rewards are immeasurable.

And not for lovers only, but for the
whole world.

You are the trip I did not take,
You are the pearls I did not buy,
You are my blue Italian lake,
You are my piece of foreign sky.

Rita Snowden

LOVE AND BE LOYAL

'If you love someone you will be loyal to him no matter what the cost. You will always believe in him, always expect the best of him, and always stand your ground in defending him.'

1 Corinthians 13:7

I believe in you
no doubt because you believe in me
which is another way of saying
whatever I have is yours
or I'm your friend
or I like your way of thinking
or thanks for standing by me
or you are something special
or I love you

Fred Bauer

A PRAYER

Lord, make me an instrument of your peace.
Where there is hatred, let me sow love;
Where there is injury, pardon;
Where there is doubt, faith;
Where there is despair, hope;
Where there is darkness, light;
Where there is sadness, joy.

O Divine Master, grant that I may not so much seek
To be consoled, as to console;
To be understood, as to understand;
To be loved, as to love.

For it is in giving that we receive;
It is in pardoning that we are pardoned;
It is in dying that we are born to eternal life.

Francis of Assisi

LOVE, JOY, PEACE...

'You have been given freedom: not freedom to do wrong, but freedom to love and serve each other. For the whole Law can be summed up in this one command: "Love others as you love yourself." ... When the Holy Spirit controls our lives he will produce this kind of fruit in us: love, joy, peace, patience, kindness, goodness, faithfulness, gentleness and self-control.'

Galatians 5:13-14, 22-23a

Joy is love singing
Peace is love resting
Patience is love enduring
Gentleness is love's touch
Goodness is love's character
Faithfulness is love's habit
Meekness is love's self-forgetfulness
Self-control is love holding the reins.

Donald Grey Barnhouse

SHARING

'Love does not consist in gazing at each other,
but looking outward together in the same
direction.'

Antoine de St Exupéry

We can share our lives together in so many
ways, and I am glad. Glad that we both like
Snoopy and chop suey, walks in the country
and listening to records. We even enjoy the
same records—most of the time. But does that
mean that we are truly sharing—'looking

outward together in the same direction'—or is there more involved? Where should we be looking and what should we be looking at?

Perhaps it means agreeing about things like where we will live and whose job comes first. Discussing how our money will be spent and when we will start a family—without fighting or trying to score points against each other. Maybe we should talk about touchy things like politics and religion. We rarely discuss what we believe, what we want out of life and why. Perhaps we don't know. Perhaps we need to share our thoughts and uncertainties. Discover together about God, about ourselves and about the path that we should walk.

A GIFT
FROM GOD

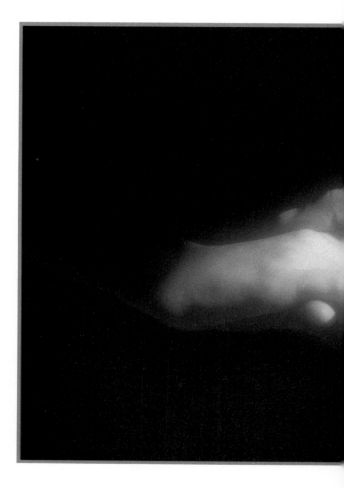

Jesus,
my friend and I live in a sex-oriented world;
we are exposed to sex everywhere;
everywhere your gift to us,
        the physical union as an act of love,
is made cheap: in films and novels
in advertising
and in the talking of people around us.

Everywhere sex seems to be more important than love
and for many love means just sex
divorced from responsibility
and from the decision to share life on a deep level.

All that is left is: make love!
and love is produced grotesquely
in one area of life and in one way
and few realize
that that can never be love.

We need you so desperately in this world
if we want to experience our relationship
as a gift from you
and if we are not to be washed away
by a wave of cheapness.

Help us
and teach us to wait for your time
before joining our bodies.

Ulrich Schaffer

LOVE
THAT LASTS

Last night we almost went too far. The
pressure has been building up for weeks. The
wanting to be alone together and the hating to
say goodnight. The excitement when we
kissed and the longing for more . . . until last
night, when we almost went too far.

Were you angry? You didn't say much.
Did you feel cheated? Did you feel that I had
led you on just for fun, and then said 'No'?
That I don't really love you?

Please try to understand. Please listen
while I tell you that it is *because* I love you so
much that I want things to be right. And
'going all the way' before we are married
would be like putting the roof on the house
before the foundations and walls are finished.

So please don't ask me to do what I feel
to be wrong, or one day I might agree. And
that agreement would damage our love,
because as well as being true to each other, we
must be true to ourselves.

Let us build our love slowly and build it
to last. Then one day we can take possession
of the house of our love with no regrets, and
enjoy it together—for always.

THE
BEST
SURPRISE
PRESENT

Today, of all days, you brought me a surprise present. Today you looked at me with love in your eyes. Today, when I was grumpy and miserable with flu: when my nose was red, my hair was a mess, and I could not even be bothered to talk.

And it was not just an ordinary present. You went ten miles in the rain, to that special shop where we had seen *the* book. The book that was so expensive that I thought that I would be lucky to have it for a combined Christmas and birthday present. I am glad that I have got the book, but more than any present I am glad that I have you.

I love you for your thoughtfulness; I love you because you were extravagant with time and money, just to bring me pleasure. Most of all I love you because you have shown me that I do not always have to be beautiful or witty or clever to earn your love. Today you showed me that you love me as I am, and that is the best surprise present of all.

'Close your heart to every love but mine;
*   hold no one in your arms but me.*
Love is as powerful as death;
*   passion is as strong as death itself.*
It bursts into flame
*   and burns like a raging fire.*
Water cannot put it out;
*   no flood can drown it.*
But if anyone tries to buy love with his wealth,
*   contempt is all he would get.'*

Song of Songs 8:6-7

BELIEVING IN LOVE

*I am becoming weak and sad in my love
because I am afraid
to become totally involved with you
—and yet
I cannot imagine a life without you.*

*I have taken you into my life
and I have moved into your life:
We have shared the ups and downs;
we have shared our innermost beings.*

*Any separation now
would be like a divorce,
even though we are not married yet,
because we have committed ourselves
to each other.*

And yet there are two conflicting feelings in me:
my love for you on the one hand
and on the other my fear of this commitment
because sometimes I doubt our love
and our strength
to endure the hardships of a life together.

But I also know
that in every certainty
there will always be some uncertainty;
that moving close to another person
is taking a risk;
that opening up is a kind of dying
and that each marriage must be a trusting in God.

I want to take that risk:
help me to believe in our love
and help me to trust God
in all our failures
because in the end
only he
can sustain our love.

Ulrich Schaffer

FOR EVER

'Diamonds are for ever'. That's what the sign on the jeweler's counter said as we stood there together, choosing the ring. 'Diamonds are for ever', and that is how we want our love to be. So we looked at diamond rings. But somehow they seemed cold and hard—they did not reflect our feelings.

'Can I show you some other stones then?' asked the jeweler. And he offered us a blood-red ruby, glowing like love's fire; a midnight-blue sapphire for love's tranquility, and then a sea-green emerald to warn against lover's jealousy. We considered them, but not one of them was perfect. None really spoke of our love.

And then I saw it. A slim gold band set with a row of tiny stones, each one a different color. The jeweler lifted it out of its white satin bed. 'This is a rather unusual ring,' he said. 'You can see that it is set with a diamond, an emerald, an amethyst, a ruby, another emerald, a sapphire and a topaz. The first letter of the name of each stone spells out a word—DEAREST.'

We did not need to talk about it. We knew without a word that this was the ring with which to seal our promise. 'Dearest for eternity'—this ring said it all.

TO WALK IN BEAUTY

*No garment is more becoming
than love. No vitamin more invigorating.
No lotion, potion, or cosmetic more
glamorizing. The exciting secret of true
beauty is love.*

*Some say that when beauty fades, love
goes. Isn't it the other way around?
Beauty only fades when love is gone.*

*If you would walk in beauty, stay
in love! You will see the loved one as
beautiful. You will see yourself as
beautiful. All the world about you will be
beautiful and the people in that world
will seem more beautiful, for they will
reflect the shining warmth and beauty
you radiate.*

Marjorie Holmes

THE SUM OF ALL MY LIFE BE LOVE

'Let love be your greatest aim.'

1 Corinthians 14:1

For love, brave love that ventureth,
For love that faileth not, I come.
For love that never wearieth,
Nor findeth burdens burdensome.

Oh Love that lightenest all my ways
Within, without, below, above,
Flow through the minutes of my days,
The sum of all my life be love.

Amy Carmichael

LOVE SONG

He called it the Love Song and he read it at their wedding. Sitting with the other guests, I took in every word.

'These words from the Bible were written to a church,' he told us, 'to a group of people who were finding it hard to get along together. Only God's love is like this all the time. But we can learn to love this way with his help. And love is the same, whether it flows between many people or just two.'

'"Love is patient and kind,"' he read, '"it is not jealous or conceited or proud; love is not ill-mannered or selfish or irritable; love does not keep a record of wrongs; love is not happy with evil, but is happy with the truth. Love never gives up; and its faith, hope, and patience never fail. Love is eternal."'

And as the words sang through the stillness, my heart whispered, 'Please God, make our love like that.'